W9-BVV-401

❖

# *Nathaniel Branden's Self-Esteem Every Day*

❖

Other books by Nathaniel Branden

*The Art of Living Consciously*
*Taking Responsibility*
*The Six Pillars of Self-Esteem*
*The Art of Self-Discovery*
*The Power of Self-Esteem*
*Judgment Day: My Years with Ayn Rand*
*How to Raise Your Self-Esteem*
*To See What I See and Know What I Know*
*Honoring the Self*
*If You Could Hear What I Cannot Say*
*What Love Asks of Us* (with Devers Branden)
*The Psychology of Romantic Love*
*The Disowned Self*
*Breaking Free*
*The Psychology of Self-Esteem*
*Who Is Ayn Rand?*

*Nathaniel Branden's*

# *Self-Esteem Every Day*

- ✤ *Reflections on*
- ✤ *Self-Esteem and*
- ✤ *Spirituality*

*A Fireside Book*
*Published by Simon & Schuster*

**F**

FIRESIDE
Rockefeller Center
1230 Avenue of the Americas
New York, NY 10020

Copyright © 1998 by The Branden Institute for Self-Esteem

All rights reserved,
including the right of reproduction
in whole or in part in any form.

FIRESIDE and colophon are registered
trademarks of Simon & Schuster Inc.

Designed by Judy Wong

Manufactured in the United States of America

1   3   5   7   9   10   8   6   4   2

Library of Congress Cataloging-in-Publication Data
Branden, Nathaniel.
[Self-esteem every day]
Nathaniel Branden's self-esteem every day : reflections on
self-esteem and spirituality.
          p.     cm.
     1. Self-esteem.      I. Title.
BF697.5.S46B746          1998
158.1—dc21          97-45895     CIP
ISBN 0-684-83338-7

*Once again, this is for Devers Branden—
with special thanks for her care and patience
in rereading almost everything I ever wrote
and highlighting the sentences that became
raw material for many of the passages in this
book.*

# Self-Esteem as a
# Spiritual Discipline

Four decades ago, when I began lecturing on self-esteem, the challenge was to persuade people that the subject was worthy of study. Almost no one was talking about self-esteem in those days. Today almost everyone seems to be talking about self-esteem, and the danger is that the idea may become trivialized.

And yet of all the judgments we pass, none is more important than the judgment we pass on ourselves: it touches the very core of our existence. Some part of us knows this. We know that more fateful by far than what others think of us is what we think of ourselves.

Although "self-esteem" is sometimes used interchangeably with "self-image," the concept runs much deeper than any "image." Self-esteem is a particular way of *experiencing* the self.

It is more complex than any mental picture of ourselves and more basic than any transitory feeling. It contains emotional, evaluative, and cognitive components. It ordinarily exists, in large measure, beneath conscious awareness, as context or container for all of our thoughts, feelings, and responses, as the ground of our being. Our responses to other people, to the challenges of work, to the sight of suffering or beauty, to the vicissitudes of life—all are affected by our deepest sense of who and what we think we are, what we are capable of, what we deserve.

Self-esteem entails certain *action dispositions:* to move toward life rather than away from it; to move toward consciousness rather than away from it; to treat facts with respect rather than avoidance or denial; to operate self-responsibly rather than the opposite. These characteristics are difficult, perhaps impossible, to fake.

What we tell ourselves about our self-esteem might be quite different from what it actually is. It might please us to believe that our self-esteem is relatively high when in fact it is seriously troubled. Nothing is more common than to deny or avoid our fears and self-doubts, thereby preventing them from ever being resolved. If I am fully willing to confront my self-esteem problems, to face and accept reality, I create the possibility of change and growth. If I deny my problems, I sentence myself to being stuck in the very pain I wish to escape. I do not wish to imply that if only we are willing to face our problems, solutions will always come easily; we might suffer from blocks we cannot overcome without professional help or might lack the knowledge that could expand our options. Nonetheless, it is safe to say that the way we respond to discomfiting realities reveals a great deal about our deepest vision of who we are— how secure or insecure we feel. It also reveals what kind of future we are likely to create for ourselves.

Of course, most people do not tell themselves anything about their self-esteem because they do not think in such terms. However, the impact of a self-estimate works its way within us whether we are aware of it or not. Ignorance of self-esteem—or misconceptions about it— does not nullify the role it plays in our lives.

Self-esteem is not the temporary euphoria or buoyancy of a drug, a compliment, or a love affair. Nor is it created by praise or by foolish and exaggerated notions of our capabilities. It is not a shallow "feel-good" phenomenon. If one does not ground it in reality, does not build it over time by operating consciously, self-responsibly, and with integrity, the result is not true self-esteem.

The essence of self-esteem is the experience that we are competent to cope with the basic challenges of life and that we are worthy of happiness. Thus, self-esteem is made of two intimately related components: (1) trust in our mind—in our ability to think and to respond effectively to challenges; and (2) confidence that success, achievement, friendship, love, respect, and personal fulfillment—in sum, *happiness*— are appropriate to us.

Self-esteem is not a luxury but a vitally important psychological need. Its survival value is obvious. To face life with assurance rather than anxiety and self-doubt is to enjoy an inestimable advantage: one's judgments and actions are less likely to be distorted and misguided. A tendency to make irrational decisions and the fear of making decisions are both observable consequences of intellectual self-distrust. To face human relationships with a benevolent, nonarrogant sense of one's own value is, again, to enjoy an advantage: self-respect evokes respect from others. A tendency to form destructive relationships—and to experience the suffering they occasion as natural or one's "destiny"—are familiar effects of feeling unlovable and without value.

Childhood experiences—or, more precisely, the way a child interprets his or her experiences—lay the foundation for the level of self-esteem that will emerge later in life. Adults who give a child a rational, noncontradictory impression of reality; who relate lovingly, respectfully, and with belief in a child's competence and worth; who avoid insults, ridicule, and emotional or physical abuse; and who uphold standards and values that inspire the best in a child—can often make the path to healthy self-esteem seem simple and natural (although not invariably or necessarily; a child's own choices and decisions should not be discounted). Adults who deal with a child in the opposite manner can make the path to self-esteem far more difficult and sometimes impossible (without some form of help).

However, what nurtures and sustains self-esteem in grown-ups is not how others deal with us but how we ourselves operate in the face of life's challenges—the choices we make and the actions we take.

In psychotherapy, work with self-esteem may have to begin with healing the psychic wounds of childhood, breaking destructive patterns of behavior, dissolving blocks, or neutralizing anxiety. But, although it can clear the ground, the elimination of negatives does not produce self-esteem. Just as the mere absence of suffering is not happiness, so the absence of anxiety is not confidence. Self-esteem is built over time by the following practices:

> *choosing consciousness* rather than uncon-
> sciousness
> *self-acceptance* rather than self-disowning
> *self-responsibility* rather than passivity, alibiing,
> or blaming
> *self-assertiveness* rather than self-suppression
> *purposefulness* rather than drifting
> *integrity* rather than self-betrayal

These practices are what I call "the six pillars of self-esteem," and I call them "practices" because I want to stress the significance of consistency and discipline. They are not things we do only when we feel like it. They represent an orientation to life akin to an ethical code. To a well-integrated person, these practices might come to feel like "second nature," but no one is born to them: they represent a spiritual achievement.

When I use the word "spiritual," I do not intend any religious, mystical, or otherworldly meaning. By "spiritual" I mean that which pertains to consciousness (as contrasted with "material," that which pertains to or is constituted of matter) and to the needs and development of consciousness. Now let me explain why I call the attainment of self-esteem a spiritual achievement.

The foundation of the practice of living consciously is respect for the facts of reality, respect for truth—recognition that that which is, is. Such a practice reflects the understanding that to place consciousness in an adversarial relationship to existence—to evade or dismiss reality—is to invite destruction. To work at cultivating such awareness within oneself is a noble pursuit, even a heroic one, because truth is sometimes frightening or painful, and the temptation to close one's eyes is sometimes strong. Whether the awareness we need to expand pertains to the external world or the world within ourselves, to strive for greater clarity of perception and understanding, to move always in the direction of heightened mindfulness, to revere truth above the avoidance of fear or pain is to commit ourselves to spiritual growth—the continuing development of our ability to see. Irrespective of any other virtues we might aspire to, this one is their foundation.

The practice of self-acceptance is the application of this virtue to oneself. Self-acceptance is realism—meaning respect for reality—about ourselves. It is the acceptance of our thoughts, emotions, and behavior—not necessarily in the sense of liking, condoning, or admiring—but in the sense of not denying or disowning. Self-acceptance is my willingness to stand in the presence of my thoughts, feelings, and actions with an attitude that makes approval or disapproval irrelevant: the desire to be aware. Obviously we will like and enjoy some aspects of who we are more than others—that is not at issue. What is at issue is whether we can be open to that which we may not like or enjoy. Perhaps I have had some embarrassing thoughts that reflect an envy or jealousy I believed I was "above"; perhaps I sometimes experience emotions that clash with my official self-concept, such as hurt or humiliation or rage; perhaps I have sometimes acted in ways that are shocking and dismaying to recall—the question is always, Can I allow space within my awareness for such realities without retreating into rationalization, denial, alibiing, or some other form of avoidance, without collapsing into self-repudiation (which is just another way of running from reality)?

Self-esteem cannot be built on a platform of self-rejection. Spiritual growth cannot emerge out of self-made blindness. The more aspects of reality a consciousness is open to seeing—and the operative word here is *seeing*, not groundless *believing*—the more highly evolved the consciousness and therefore the most mature the level of spiritual development.

In understanding the practice of self-responsibility, let us begin with the observation that the natural development of a human being is from dependence to independence, from helplessness to increasing efficacy, from nonresponsibility to personal accountability. Self-responsibility means that we recognize first that we are the authors of our choices and actions; and second that we are responsible for our well-being and for the attainment of our desires; and third that if we wish to gain values from others, we must offer values in exchange: no one exists merely to take care of us, no other human being is our property. The most fundamental expression of self-responsibility is reliance on our own minds—the choice to think and to operate consciously—as opposed to living second-hand, through values and judgments borrowed from others.

Independence in the full sense does not come easily to most people. What many call "thinking" is merely a recycling of others' thoughts and opinions. To look at the world through one's own eyes, to be willing to live by one's own judgment, requires courage, self-trust, and intellectual honesty—in a word, integrity, a spiritual virtue.

To many self-assertiveness might seem like the very opposite of a spiritual virtue. Yet, if the practice of self-assertiveness is considered, not in a vacuum, torn from all context, but as part of a network of virtues that include rationality, self-responsibility, and integrity, it may be viewed in a very different light, as an essential step toward the realization of our humanity. Self-assertiveness is not about running over widows and orphans to get to the front of the line or being rude to waiters or behaving as though no one's needs existed but one's own: it is, rather, the courage to treat oneself and one's convictions with decent respect in encounters with other persons; the willingness to stand up for one's ideas and to live one's values; the honesty to let oneself be visible to others—or, to say it differently, not to be so controlled by fear of someone's disapproval that one twists one's true self out of recognizable form. Thus defined, we can see that self-assertiveness is not self-indulgence but is among the rarest of virtues. Certainly spirituality is closer to openness than self-concealment, to candor than dissembling, to authenticity than its opposite.

The practice of living purposefully, as opposed to passively drifting through life, is essential to any genuine sense of control over one's existence. It is our goals and purposes that give our days their focus. To live purposefully is to think through and formulate one's short-term and long-term goals or purposes, to identify the actions needed to realize them, to keep oneself on track, and to pay careful attention to whether the outcomes produced by one's actions are the outcomes anticipated or whether one needs to go back to the drawing board. To act only on the whim of the moment or on the basis of the chance encounter, invitation, or opportunity is to embrace helplessness as one's fundamental response: to be not a thoughtful initiator but only an impulsive reactor. To remove oneself from the realm of purpose is to become a non-participant, to exist on the sidelines of life where no form of spirituality is possible.

The practice of integrity entails congruence between what we know, what we profess, and what we do. To be loyal in action to one's under-standing and professed convictions is the essence of integrity. When there is not congruence but contradiction, at some level consciousness is betraying itself. If one is genuinely concerned with the growth and evolution of consciousness, which is what a spiritual quest or commitment entails, then a lack of integrity cannot be toler-ated: it is a self-inflicted wound one must strive to heal. If we torment our mate with small or large lies and inconsistencies, are cruel to our children, or are dishonorable with our associates, colleagues, or customers—if we run from honest self-examination while protesting that it is our highest concern—we cannot then renew our purchase on spirituality by studying the *I Ching,* the Kabbala, the Bible, or the scriptures of Buddhism. The issue is not so much whether we are perfect in our integrity but rather how concerned we are to correct any breaches in it. In the absence of such concern, whatever our life's journey is about, it is not about spiritual growth.

I began thinking about the relationship between self-esteem and spirituality some years ago when I was asked a provocative question by an elderly businessman. I was addressing a group of CEOs on the ideas I was writing about in *The Six Pillars of Self-Esteem.* I was talking about the practice of living consciously, self-acceptance, self-responsibility, self-assertiveness, living purposefully, and personal integrity—and why they were the foundations of self-esteem. At the end of my presentation, the oldest businessman in the group said to me, "Is this a religion—these principles?" At first I was puzzled since I had made no reference to religion and no such thought was in my mind. Seeing the puzzled expression on my face, he corrected himself: "Perhaps what I mean to ask is, is this a code of ethics?" I answered, "Well, I hadn't quite been thinking of it that way, but now that you ask, yes, I would say it is—or part of one. After all, it's not surprising that the virtues that self-esteem asks of us are also the virtues that life asks of us." Afterward, I found myself reflecting on why he had first thought of religion. Was it simply that for many people religion and ethics are almost synonymous? Somehow, in this case, I did not think so. What I began to suspect much later was that he had been groping for the connection that I have made explicit in this essay: the connection between the six pillars and spirituality.

For many people one of the commonest associations with the idea of spirituality is the longing to feel at home in the universe—to feel benevolently connected to all that exists and to the ultimate source, whatever that might be, of all that exists. We will not, in this context, raise the troublesome question of whether we wish to be benevolently connected to that which we regard as evil: instead, we will focus just on the longing for the experience of peace and harmony with existence, in the most profound sense imaginable.

Whatever else may be required for the fulfillment of this desire, inner peace and harmony with oneself are preconditions of peace and harmony with the external world. A spirit cannot be benevolently connected to the universe before being benevolently connected to itself. However, there is a sense in which the reverse is also true. The relationship is reciprocal. A spirit at loggerheads with reality cannot be at peace with itself. That is why the theme of respect for the facts of reality runs through my discussion of all six pillars. That which is, is; that which is not, is not. No truth is more fundamental. To embrace this truth is the beginning of self-esteem. It is also the beginning of spiritual development.

One final word. The purpose of the sayings that follow this essay—one for each day of the year—is not to serve as a substitute for a serious study of self-esteem. Rather, the sayings are offered as a point of focus to assist you in maintaining the consistency and discipline that healthy self-esteem requires. They can provoke, inspire, remind, and serve as objects of meditation. Their purpose is to help keep the fire lit.

❖

*Nathaniel Branden's*
*Self-Esteem Every Day*

❖

# January

## January 1

There are two questions that all human beings, with rare exceptions, ask themselves quite often. The rare exceptions are the persons who know the answer to the first of these questions, at least to a significant extent. But everyone asks the second, sometimes in wonder, sometimes in despair. These are the two questions: How am I to understand myself? How am I to understand other people? To both questions the principles of self-esteem provide an important key. If you know what a person ties his self-esteem to, you can understand a good deal about his motivation.

## January 2

The "I," the ego, the deepest self, is the faculty of awareness, the ability to think. Across a lifetime, knowledge grows, convictions may change, emotions come and go; but that which knows, judges, and feels—that is the changeless constant within us.

## January 3

The drama of our lives is the external reflection of our internal vision of ourselves—of our competence and worth.

## January 4

None of us can be indifferent to our own self-evaluation—just as we cannot be indifferent to the face we see in the mirror.

## January 5

Although most of us do not experience this directly, the "self" we are esteeming—or not esteeming—is our mind: our ability to think and to cope with the challenges of life.

## January 6

Self-esteem is always a matter of degree. I have never known anyone who was entirely lacking in self-esteem, nor have I known anyone who was incapable of growing in self-esteem.

## January 7

If self-esteem is not reality-based, if it is not rooted in such virtues as rationality, self-responsibility, and integrity, it is not self-esteem.

❖   ❖   ❖   ❖   ❖

## January 8

It is foolish to equate any experience of "feeling good" with self-esteem. All sorts of things can make you "feel good"—for the moment.

## January 9

Self-esteem is a particular way of *experiencing the self*. Its two components are self-efficacy and self-respect. Self-efficacy is the experience of competence in thinking, learning, making appropriate decisions, and responding effectively to the challenges of life. Self-respect is the experience that success, achievement, love, joy, fulfillment—in a word, *happiness*—are natural and appropriate to us.

## January 10

To provide a formal definition: self-esteem is the disposition to experience oneself as competent to cope with the challenges of life and as worthy of happiness.

## January 11

Self-esteem is an intimate experience. It resides in the core of your being. It is what you think and feel about yourself, not what someone else thinks or feels about you.

## January 12

You can be loved by your family, your mate, and your friends yet not love yourself. You can be admired by your associates yet regard yourself as worthless. You can project an image of assurance and poise that fools almost everyone yet secretly tremble with a sense of inadequacy. You can fulfill the expectations of others yet fail your own. You can win every honor yet feel that you have accomplished nothing. What shall it profit a person to gain the esteem of the whole world yet lose his or her own?

## January 13

If self-esteem is the judgment that one is appropriate to life—if self-esteem is self-affirming consciousness, a mind that trusts itself—no one can generate this experience except oneself. Others can support one's self-esteem but they cannot create it.

## January 14

A sure sign of troubled self-esteem is the delusion that self-esteem can be acquired as a free gift from others.

When we appreciate the true nature of self-esteem, we see that it is not competitive or comparative. It is not about making myself higher by making you lower. It has nothing to do with you. It is joy in my own being.

Arrogance, boastfulness, and the overestimation of our abilities reflects underdeveloped self-esteem rather than, as some people imagine, too much self-esteem.

Sometimes people ask, "Can a person have too much self-esteem?" Can a person have too much physical health? In both cases, the answer is no.

## January 18

Self-esteem and grandiosity are not on a continuum; grandiosity is not "excessive self-esteem" but a compensatory defense mechanism for lack of self-esteem.

## January 19

To say that self-esteem is a basic need is to say
(1) that it makes an essential contribution to
life; (2) that it is indispensable to normal and
healthy development; and (3) that it has survival
value.

## January 20

If you face life without confidence in your own powers, you succumb too easily to setbacks and adversity; you lack the will to persevere.

If you face life without the conviction that you have a right to be happy, you will not fight for your happiness.

❖ ❖ ❖ ❖ ❖

## January 22

In the nature of our existence, we must act to achieve values. And in order to act appropriately, we must value the beneficiary of our actions. In order to seek values, we must consider ourselves worthy of enjoying them. In order to fight for our happiness, we must consider ourselves worthy of happiness. Many people put up with a life of suffering because they feel they deserve no better.

## January 23

The greatest barrier to achievement and success is not lack of talent or ability but rather the feeling that achievement and success, above a certain level, are outside our self-concept—our image of who we are and what is appropriate to us. The greatest barrier to love is the secret fear that we are unlovable. The greatest barrier to happiness is the wordless sense that happiness is not our proper destiny.

## January 24

The level of our self-esteem creates a set of implicit expectations about what is possible and appropriate to us. These expectations engender the actions that turn them into realities. And the realities then confirm and strengthen the original beliefs. Self-esteem—high or low—is a generator of self-fulfilling prophecies.

## January 25

Some enthusiasts of self-esteem believe good self-esteem solves nearly all the important problems of life. This is untrue. Struggle is intrinsic to life. Sooner or later everyone experiences anxiety and pain—and while self-esteem can make one less susceptible, it cannot make one impervious.

## January 26

Think of self-esteem as *the immune system of consciousness*. If you have a healthy immune system, you might still become ill, but you are less likely to; if you do become ill, you will likely recover faster—your resilience is greater. Similarly, if you have high self-esteem, you might still know times of emotional suffering, but less often and with faster recovery—your resilience is greater. A well-developed sense of self is a necessary if not sufficient condition of your well-being. Its presence does not guarantee fulfillment, but its absence guarantees some measure of anxiety, frustration, or despair.

## January 27

Do you know which of your actions have a positive effect on your self-esteem? Do you know which ones have a negative effect?

## January 28

Your choices have psychological consequences. The way you choose to deal with reality, truth, facts—your choice to honor or dishonor your own perceptions—registers in your mind, for good or for bad, and either confirms and strengthens your self-esteem or undermines and weakens it.

The will to efficacy is the refusal to identify your ego or self with momentary feelings of inadequacy or defeat. It is impressive to see a person who has been battered by life in many ways, who is torn by a variety of unsolved problems, who may be alienated from many aspects of the self—but who is still fighting, still struggling, still striving to find the path to a fulfilling existence, moved by the wisdom of knowing, "I am more than my problems."

## January 30

One of the core meanings of enlightenment is liberation from false and spurious value attachments that blind you to your true essence. When and if I learn that I am ultimately my mind and my manner of using it; when and if I understand that ego is only the internal experience of consciousness, the ultimate center of awareness, I am free.

## January 31

Working on one's self-esteem is working on the relationship of one's consciousness to reality. This is the ultimate spiritual project.

# *February*

## February 1

To accept struggle as part of life, to accept all of it, even the darkest moments of anguish; to be motivated by love rather than fear, by confidence rather than insecurity: these are the benchmarks of high self-esteem. The wish to avoid fear and pain is not the motive that drives the lives of highly evolved men and women: rather it is the life force within them, thrusting toward its unique form of expression—the actualization of personal values.

## February 2

Poor self-esteem does not necessarily render you incapable of achieving any real values. Some people may have the talent, energy, and drive to achieve a great deal in spite of feelings of inadequacy or unworthiness—like the highly productive workaholic who is driven to prove his worth to, say, a father who predicted he would never amount to anything. But it does mean that you will be severely restricted in your ability to enjoy your achievements. Nothing you do will ever feel like enough.

## February 3

The feeling that "I am enough" does not mean that I have nothing to learn, nothing further to achieve, and nowhere to grow to. It means that I accept myself, that I am not on trial in my own eyes, that I value and respect myself. This is not an act of indulgence but of courage.

❖ ❖ ❖ ❖ ❖

When parents ask what they can do to support the growth of self-esteem in their children, I emphasize the importance of cultivating their own self-esteem. They must work on becoming and exemplifying that which they wish to teach.

## *February 5*

Research tells us that one of the best ways to get a head start toward self-esteem is to have parents with good self-esteem. When children see what serene confidence and self-respect look like, they are more likely to internalize such attitudes, believing that this is how human beings are meant to be.

## February 6

Parents cannot "give" a child self-esteem. No one can. But they can make the road to self-esteem immeasurably easier—by treating a child not only with love but also with respect and acceptance, by communicating confidence in the child's competence and moral and intellectual capabilities, by providing appropriate guidance, by upholding reasonable expectations that inspire rather than oppress, and by giving a child the experience of living in a rational universe.

## February 7

Children whose thoughts and feelings are taken
seriously and treated with respect tend to trust
themselves, believe in themselves, and respond
to challenges with confidence.

## February 8

Children who are loved and respected by parents who see them *realistically* (and not as angels or saints) usually experience themselves as lovable and as deserving of respect. An important consequence is that as adults they will be much less likely to tolerate abuse from others. They will treat others decently and require that others treat them decently.

## February 9

Children who are raised with rational expectations (not based on a parent's neurotic needs) tend to hold rational expectations for themselves.

## February 10

One of the most important issues in a child's development is what parents do when they see the child making mistakes. Do parents teach that mistakes are reprehensible or that they are normal and are to be learned from so that they will not be repeated in the future?

## February 11

One of the most important issues for anyone's self-esteem is one's reaction to one's own mistakes. Are they treated with self-blame or even self-damnation—or as opportunities for learning and growth?

## *February 12*

If you are terrified of making mistakes, you will be reluctant to acknowledge them when you do make them—and therefore you will not correct them.

For children mastery entails struggle. This means they must be *permitted* to struggle. If parents inappropriately step in to "help"—out of impatience or solicitude—they sabotage important learning. Among other things, the child is unlikely to discover the advantages of perseverance and self-discipline.

## *February 14*

One of the most significant yet rarely recorded traumas in a child's life is the discovery of how common it is for adults to lie. This can undermine a child's sense of reality—respect for the distinction between the real and the unreal. It can also instill the idea that lying is normal.

## February 15

If you want to teach your children honesty, do not punish them for telling the truth.

If parents do everything right, it does not follow *necessarily* that their children will grow up with healthy self-esteem. Life is more complex than that. Children play an active role in their own development; they are not merely passive clay molded by biology and environment. Parents' behavior can be impeccable, yet the child might grow up insecure and self-doubting. Sometimes parents who seemingly do everything wrong, rear children who do well in school, form good relationships, operate self-responsibly, and give all the evidence of having a good level of self-esteem. It is almost as if these children were put on earth to drive psychologists crazy. But it would be irresponsible for any parent to count on having one of these "invulnerables."

So long as children continue to struggle, so long as they do not give up the will to understand, to make sense out of their experience, they are psychologically safe, no matter what their anguish or bewilderment: they keep their mind and their desire for efficacy intact. When they surrender the possibility of achieving efficacy, they surrender the possibility of achieving full self-esteem.

## February 18

Children who cling tenaciously to the will to understand may suffer enormously in the early years if they are caught in an irrational environment, but in the deepest sense they will survive psychologically: they will continue struggling to find their way to the rational view of life that should have been exemplified by their elders, but wasn't; they will doubtless feel alienated from many of the people around them—and legitimately so; but they will not feel alienated from reality. They will not feel that it is they who are incompetent to live.

## February 19

No one was ever made good by being informed he or she is bad.

Just as one of the greatest gifts a parent can give a child is projection of a belief in the child's competence and worth, so one of the greatest gifts you can offer another human being is not to buy at face value his or her negative self-esteem.

## February 21

What a great parent, a great teacher, a great coach, and a great psychotherapist all have in common is the ability to see a potential in a person that the person does not see—and to be relentless in projecting that vision.

## February 22

While we do not know all the biological or developmental factors that may influence self-esteem, we know a good deal about the specific (volitional) practices that raise or lower it. We know that an honest commitment to understanding inspires self-trust and that an avoidance of the effort has the opposite effect. We know that people who live mindfully feel more competent than those who live mindlessly. We know that self-responsibility and integrity engender self-respect and that the opposite behavior does not.

## February 23

One of the forms of psychological heroism that builds self-esteem is the willingness to tolerate anxiety and uncertainty in the pursuit of your values—whether those values be work goals, the love of another human being, raising a family, or personal growth.

❖   ❖   ❖   ❖   ❖

The person with poor self-esteem acts out of fear rather than confidence. Not to live but to escape the anxiety of living becomes the basic goal. Not creativity but safety becomes the ruling desire. The gravitational pull of these feelings must be overcome if such a person is to rise.

## *February 25*

A strong sense of personal identity is the product of two things: independent thinking and the possession of an integrated set of values.

## February 26

When a person of high self-esteem and independence meets another person for the first time, the first question is normally not What does this person think of me? but rather What do *I* think of this person?

## February 27

When you have self-esteem, you expect others to *perceive* your value, not *create* it. When you have low self-esteem, you imagine that if only others value you, *then* you will value yourself. But waiting for Godot is not a good idea—not if you genuinely wish to earn self-admiration.

The higher your self-esteem, the better equipped you are to cope with life's adversities—the more resilient you are, the more you resist pressure to succumb to despair. The higher your self-esteem, the more likely you are to be creative and successful in your work. The higher your self-esteem, the more ambitious you tend to be, not necessarily in a career or financial sense, but in terms of what you hope to experience in life—emotionally, creatively, and spiritually. The higher your self-esteem, the more likely you are to form nourishing rather than destructive relationships, since like is drawn to like, health is attracted to health, and vitality and expansiveness are more appealing than emptiness, dependency, or exploitativeness. The higher your self-esteem, the more inclined you are to treat others with respect, benevolence, and goodwill, since you do not perceive them as threats and since self-respect is the foundation of respect for others. The higher your self-esteem, the more joy you experience in the sheer fact of being, of waking up in the morning, of living inside your body.

❖   ❖   ❖   ❖   ❖   89

## February 29

Self-esteem is the state of those at war neither with themselves nor others.

❖

# *March*

❖

## March 1

As an adult, you must take responsibility for your self-esteem. It is too late to lament, "If only Mother and Father had been different." It is also futile.

## March 2

How can you raise the level of your self-esteem?
First you must learn to live consciously—
because that is the foundation of everything.

## March 3

Living consciously means being mentally active rather than passive. It is the ability to look at the world through fresh eyes. It is intelligence taking joy in its own function. Living consciously is seeking to be aware of everything that bears on our interests, actions, values, purposes, and goals. It is the willingness to confront facts, pleasant or unpleasant. It is the desire to discover our mistakes and correct them. Within the range of our interests and concerns, it is the quest to keep expanding our awareness and understanding, both of the world outside and the world within. It is respect for reality and for the distinction between the real and the unreal. It is the commitment to see what we see and know what we know. It is recognition of the fact that the act of dismissing reality is the root of all evil.

## March 4

Have you ever noticed that even though your interests would be served by heeding certain realities, you will not necessarily do so? Or that you do not necessarily think about the things you should think about or confront facts that urgently require your attention? Have you ever noticed that you have the option of turning the light of consciousness brighter or dimmer—and that you do not necessarily make the appropriate choice? This is the meaning of free will—the choice to focus awareness or not to, to think or not to, to operate consciously in any moment or not to.

## March 5

The choices you make about your degree of consciousness do not vanish, leaving no trace; they have long-term consequences, not only in how well your life works but also in how you feel about yourself—whether you are a person you can admire.

## March 6

Intellectual sovereignty, self-reliance, and self-responsibility are rooted in a firm sense of reality. This means a deep respect for facts. What is, is. Things are what they are. Truth is not obliterated by the refusal to see it. Facts are not annihilated by the pretense that they do not exist.

## *March 7*

Our minds are our basic means of survival. All our distinctively human accomplishments are the reflections of our ability to think. Successful life depends on the appropriate use of intelligence—appropriate, that is, to our self-assigned tasks and goals and their attendant challenges.

## March 8

The more intelligent you are, the greater is your potential for awareness, but the principle of living consciously holds irrespective of the degree of intelligence. Living consciously means generating a level of awareness that is equal to the task before you—whether it be designing a computer program or sweeping the floor.

## *March 9*

Thinking for yourself, thinking independently—about work, your relationships, and the values that guide your life—is an essential part of living consciously.

## *March 10*

You are not moved to change those things whose reality you deny.

## March 11

Merely choosing to think is truly heroic in some cases. For instance, if you choose to think and you come up against facts you cannot handle, what then? If you choose to think and your thinking leads to conclusions that threaten to disrupt the routine of your life, what then? If you choose to think and your conclusions lead you far from the mainstream beliefs of others, what then? If you choose to think and you begin noticing traits and characteristics of yourself you do not admire, what then? If you choose to think and you see what you do not wish to see, or what others do not wish you to see, what then? Your long-term interests may best be served by remaining conscious, but that is not how it may *feel* in the moment—which is why I speak of the heroism of living consciously.

## *March 12*

All of us tend to operate more consciously in some areas than in others. Notice that the areas where you operate most consciously are also the areas where your life works best.

## March 13

Any time you admit a difficult truth, any time you face that which you have been afraid to face, any time you acknowledge, to yourself or to others, facts you have been evading, any time you are willing to tolerate temporary fear or anxiety on the path to better contact with reality—your self-esteem increases.

## March 14

You undermine your self-esteem when you persist in your evasions and contradictions, because at a deeper level you *know what you are doing.*

## March 15

Rationality—respect for the facts of reality—
must include respect for the facts of your own
being. Your inner world, too, is part of reality.
No one can be said to be living consciously who
exempts self-awareness and self-examination
from the agenda.

## March 16

What you are blind to in the world tends to reflect what you are blind to in yourself. A person who denies the presence of a need tends to be blind to opportunities to satisfy that need—as, for instance, when a person denies his need and desire for companionship, suffers loneliness, and does not see opportunities for friendship. Denying the reality of pain breeds oblivion to the source of the pain and thus continual exposure to new hurt—as when a woman repeatedly subjects herself to exploitative and enervating encounters with men.

## March 17

Often, a flight from reality is a flight from the reality of your inner state, the thoughts and feelings you are frightened to face or understand.

❖ ❖ ❖ ❖ ❖

## *March 18*

Among the many crimes committed against the younger generation, one of the worst is that young people are taught next to nothing about reason, rationality, or the importance of critical thinking.

## March 19

The quest of reason is for *the noncontradictory integration of experience.*

❖    ❖    ❖    ❖    ❖

## March 20

One of the meanings of living consciously is paying attention to what works and doing more of it and trying to understand the principles involved. And also paying attention to what doesn't work, *and not doing it.*

## *March 21*

The question is, Do you invest your activities with your keenest consciousness, or do you settle for something less than that?

❖   ❖   ❖   ❖   ❖

## March 22

When you are frightened, you typically pull energy *in* to your center, seeing less, hearing less—shrinking consciousness precisely when you need to *expand* it.

## March 23

A simple application of living consciously is taking responsibility for the words coming out of your mouth.

## March 24

If you are wise enough to base your self-esteem not on being "right" but on being rational—on being conscious—and on having integrity, then you recognize that acknowledgment and correction of an error is not an abyss into which you have fallen but a height you can take pride in having climbed.

## March 25

One of the ways you convey respect for another human being is through the consciousness you bring to the encounter—through seeing, hearing, and responding in a way that allows him or her to feel understood.

## March 26

If you are willing to stay fully present to your emotions without denial or disowning, the typical result is not the collapse of lucidity but its enhancement. In other words, feel deeply to think clearly.

## March 27

If you bring more consciousness to what you do when you are afraid or angry, you will see that *other options exist.*

## March 28

Living consciously entails the question, What are the *grounds* of belief? What is the *evidence*?

## March 29

The need to live consciously has acquired a new urgency in the modern age. The more rapid the rate of change, the more dangerous it is to live mechanically, relying on routines of belief and behavior that may be irrelevant or obsolete.

## March 30

The age of the muscle-worker is past; this is the age of the mind-worker. That your mind is your basic tool of survival is not new; what is new is that this fact has become inescapably clear. The market is rapidly diminishing for people who have nothing to contribute but physical labor. An economy in which knowledge, information, creativity—and their translation into innovation—are the prime sources of wealth demands *minds*, people who are able and willing to *think*.

## *March 31*

Whoever continually strives to achieve a clearer
and clearer vision of reality and our place in it,
whoever is pulled forward by a *passion* for such
clarity is, to that extent, leading a spiritual life.

# *April*

## April 1

If you deny and disown pieces of who you are—
your thoughts, feelings, or actions—because
they do not fit your official self-concept, you
damage your self-esteem. You send yourself a
message that who you really are is not good
enough.

## April 2

Self-esteem is impossible without self-acceptance. But self-acceptance is not an easy idea for most people to understand. They confuse acceptance with liking, condoning, or even admiring. Yet acceptance does not imply any of these things; it means awareness without critical judgment or condemnation. It means not denying or fighting reality. It means respect for the facts of your own being. It means saying, I'm not happy that I had that thought, but yes, I accept the fact that I had it. It means, I'm not pleased to have these feelings, but I acknowledge them as mine and allow myself to look at and experience them. It means, I am not proud of that behavior, but yes, it was I who did what I did. When you open yourself to reality—even when the reality is painful—you make yourself stronger.

## April 3

Self-acceptance does not ask, Do I like it or not? It asks, Is this true of me or not? It does not ask, Will this be true of me forever? It asks, Was it ever true of me—ever an expression of me—even for a moment?

## April 4

To be self-accepting does not mean to be without a desire to change, improve, or grow. Self-acceptance has nothing to do with complacency. The paradox is, self-acceptance is a precondition of change. If you cannot accept the fact that those unwanted thoughts occurred to you, how can you think about or learn from them? If you cannot accept the fact that you have these distressing emotions, how can you resolve to grow beyond them? If you cannot accept the fact that you have been acting unconsciously, how will you learn to act more consciously?

## April 5

In one of my therapy groups, a woman grew angry with me and said, "You're always talking about self-acceptance. But I've got lousy self-esteem. Am I supposed to *accept* that?" I answered, "If you don't accept the fact that right now your self-esteem is low, how do you think you will learn to raise it? Do you think you will do better for yourself if you deny the reality of the problem? All that accomplishes is to leave you stuck."

## April 6

This is the principle of self-acceptance: Do not be an adversary to your own experience.

## *April 7*

The challenge of self-acceptance is not confined to acknowledging faults. You can be as frightened of your assets as of your shortcomings. Some of us are afraid to accept our own intelligence, ambition, excitement, or beauty. We might be afraid that these traits will alienate us from others or invite their envy and hostility.

❖ ❖ ❖ ❖ ❖

## *April 8*

Out of fear of someone's animosity or disapproval, you can betray the best within yourself.
You may repress not your lowest but your highest. What is left behind is some vague, inarticu-
late sense of having committed treason.

## April 9

Can you accept the self you were at an earlier stage of your development? Can you accept the child you once were, or the teenager, without embarrassment or repudiation? Or are you relentlessly unforgiving toward any self that knew less and was less than the you of today?

## *April 10*

If you condemn all your earlier selves—all the earlier stages of your development—who gets the credit for bringing you to where you are today?

## *April 11*

When you learn to "forgive" (though there is nothing to forgive) the child you once were for what he or she didn't know, or couldn't do, or couldn't cope with; when you understand and accept that that child was struggling to survive as best he or she could—then your adult self is no longer an adversary of your child self. One part of you is not at war with another part. Then you enhance your inner harmony—and therefore your self-esteem.

## *April 12*

An attitude of basic self-acceptance is what an effective psychotherapist tries to awaken in a person of even the lowest self-esteem. This attitude can inspire an individual to face whatever he or she most dreads to encounter within, free of self-hatred and self-repudiation that can sap the will to live. It entails the declaration, I choose to value myself, to treat myself with respect, to stand up for my right to exist. This is a yet deeper level of acceptance than the acceptance of some disturbing thought, feeling, or action. This is where self-esteem begins.

## *April 13*

You cannot forgive yourself for an action you
cannot acknowledge having taken.

## April 14

When you fight a block or a resistance, it grows stronger. When you acknowledge, accept, and experience it fully, it begins to melt.

## April 15

Self-acceptance entails the idea of compassion, of being a friend to yourself—of trying to understand where you were coming from when you did something of which you are now ashamed.

## April 16

Self-acceptance is, quite simply, realism. That which is, is. That which you think, you think. That which you feel, you feel. That which you did, you did.

## April 17

Some people think it is a virtue to disown parts of themselves of which they disapprove. But they only mire themselves in those parts forever. They have cut off the only means of growth or transformation.

## *April 18*

There is a physical aspect to self-acceptance, just as there is to self-rejection. Watch a child fight not to feel what he is feeling. He tightens his chest and constricts his breathing. That is also what adults do. When you deny and disown the first thing you do is stop breathing. When you accept, you relax and breathe—you open, you do not shut down.

A child says, "I hate Grandma!" A parent answers, "Wow! *Right now* you are really feeling mad at Grandma! Want to tell me about it?" The parent is teaching self-acceptance. In a moment or two, the child's anger will most likely be gone. A child says, "I hate Grandma!" A parent answers, "What a terrible thing to say! You don't mean it! What's the matter with you?" The parent is teaching repression, self-rejection, and self-alienation. The anger is driven underground to fester.

## April 20

In one of his books, the philosopher Nietzsche has a wonderful line that bears on the issue of self-acceptance. It goes something like this: "'I did it,' says memory. 'I couldn't have,' says pride, and remains inexorable. Eventually, memory yields." So, paraphrasing, "I feel it," says perception. "I couldn't be," says an insecure self, "I'm not that kind of person." Perception answers, "My mistake."

## April 21

Your liabilities pose the problem of inadequacy; your assets pose the problem of responsibility. Both can tempt you into self-disowning.

## *April 22*

Suppose you feel you *cannot* accept some fact about yourself. Then own your refusal to accept. Own the block. Embrace it fully. And watch it begin to disappear. The principle is this: Begin where you are—accept *that*. Then change and growth become possible.

## April 23

I once heard a wife, in a moment of great anger, say to her husband, "Right now I feel that I hate you." I was filled with admiration for the precision of her language and the consciousness she retained even under stress. What a difference between saying "Right now I feel that I hate you" and simply saying "I hate you." She did not deny her emotion—she honored her anger—but she did not forget that she loved this man or that their relationship transcended this one moment.

## April 24

It is very difficult to accept in others emotions
you cannot accept in yourself.

## April 25

The motives you disown in yourself you will project onto others.

## April 26

Sometimes you complain that others have rejected you, oblivious to the fact that you have rejected them.

## April 27

If you fully accepted what you think is the darkest side of yourself, in the end you would love yourself more, not less—and you would deserve to, because you would no longer be fighting reality.

## April 28

It is easier to accept your impulses if you know you do not necessarily have to act on them. You exercise judgment. You make choices.

## April 29

Often you begin disowning pieces of yourself to win someone else's approval; then you continue the process to win your own. You immortalize those who would not accept you as you were by giving their perspective permanent residence within your psyche. It is time to reclaim your disowned self.

## April 30

Daily work at self-acceptance is a challenging spiritual task. That is one reason it is so rarely done. But if you have the self-discipline to persevere, you will discover that true self-acceptance is the opposite of, and much harder than, any self-indulgence. It is a path to enlightenment.

# *May*

## May 1

One characteristic of children is that they are almost entirely dependent on others. They look to others to fulfill most of their needs. As they mature, they increasingly rely on their own efforts. One characteristic of successfully evolved adults is that they learn to take responsibility for their own lives—physically, emotionally, intellectually, and spiritually. This practice of self-responsibility is one of the pillars of self-esteem.

## May 2

In a world in which we are exposed to more information, more options, more philosophies, more perspectives than ever before, in which we must *choose* the values by which we will live (rather than unquestioningly follow some tradition for no better reason than that our parents did), we need to be willing to stand on our own judgment and trust our own intelligence—to look at the world through our own eyes—to chart our course and *think through* how to achieve the future we want, to commit ourselves to continuous questioning and learning—to be, in a word, self-responsible.

## May 3

If you wish to be self-responsible, you must be willing to make yourself the cause of the effects you want rather than hoping or demanding that someone else "do something" while your own contribution is to wait and suffer.

## May 4

When you are self-responsible, you recognize that you are the author of your choices and actions.

## May 5

"I couldn't help it!" seems to be the most popular theme song of our day. It echoes the pronouncements of many of our social scientists that no one can help anything. Apart from the fact that this belief is false, it generates incalculable harmful social consequences. The abandonment of personal accountability makes self-esteem, as well as decent and benevolent social relationships, impossible. At its worst, it becomes a license to kill. If you want a world that works, you need a culture of accountability.

## *May 6*

Taking on responsibilities that properly belong to someone else means behaving irresponsibly toward yourself. You need to know where you end and someone else begins. You need to understand boundaries. You need to know what is and is not up to you, what is and is not in your control, what is and is not your responsibility.

## May 7

If you are an adult, you are responsible for your life and well-being. No one owes you the fulfillment of your needs or wants; no one is here on earth to serve you. If you respect the principle of self-ownership, you understand that no one else owns you and that you do not own anyone else. Only on this understanding can there be peace on earth and good will among human beings.

## *May 8*

If you want the cooperation of others in the pursuit of your goals, you must appeal to their interests and needs; you must offer them values of some kind; your wants per se are not a claim on anyone.

## May 9

If you choose not to live self-responsibly, you count on others to make up your default. No one abjures self-responsibility on a desert island.

## May 10

You are responsible for the level of consciousness you bring to your activities—whether driving your car, listening to your child, talking to a customer, reading a book, or choosing your spouse.

## May 11

The first act of self-responsibility is the choice
to think.

## May 12

Thought is not infallible; it can lead to error. If we act on our error, we may suffer pain or defeat. And it will be our responsibility, our "fault." If we act on our own judgment and are mistaken, we cannot reasonably pass the buck to anyone else. Whereas—and this is the great temptation for some people—if you forgo independence and let others decide, the error or disaster is not your responsibility, and you are not to blame (or so you tell yourself). You are off the hook. So here is one of the great choices and challenges of life. Self-responsibility is for grown-ups.

## *May 13*

A policy of independent thinking can bring us into conflict with the opinions of others. And then the question becomes, What matters more to you: your own perception of reality or someone else's approval? If this is not a spiritual issue, what is?

## May 14

If you accept the principle of self-responsibility, you recognize that the achievement of your happiness is no one's task but your own. In a love relationship, you will have the opportunity to *share* your happiness, not have someone who is there to "make" you happy.

## May 15

If you do not grow into proper independence, never learn to think for yourself, there is a void within you. Your need for knowledge remains, as does your need for guiding principles of action. Inevitably, you turn to others to fill these needs. You feel, wordlessly, that you do not know, that other seem to know; somehow they have plumbed that mysterious unknowable: reality. Therefore, if others are favorably impressed by you, the you must be a worthy person. You feel, What other standard of self-esteem can there be? So others hold your sense of worth in their hands.

## May 16

Nothing is more common in irrational moments than obliterating your awareness that you have chosen to do what you are doing; you regard the action as if it were somehow happening of its own accord. Do you want to grow in self-esteem? *Own* your actions. Take conscious responsibility for what you are doing *while you are doing it*. For example, when sleeping with someone you would be ashamed to be seen with, do not tell yourself, This really isn't me. Or when striking your child, do not tell yourself, I'm not myself. You will learn that there are actions you are unable to permit yourself once you take full responsibility for doing what you do.

As regards fear of others' disapproval, the problem is not that you want to be liked. Who does not prefer being liked to being disliked? The problem is where this desire stands in your hierarchy of values. Does it stand at the peak, above integrity and self-esteem? The issue is not whether you want to be liked but what you are willing to give in exchange. Are you willing to give up the integrity of your judgment? The tragedy for many people is that their answer is *yes*. I call this a tragedy because so much suffering is traceable to this surrender.

## May 18

The more you surrender to the fear of someone's disapproval, the more you lose face in
your own eyes, and the more desperate you
become for *someone's* approval. Within you is a
void that should have been filled by self-esteem.
When you attempt to fill it with the approval of
others instead, the void grows deeper and the
hunger for acceptance and approval grows
stronger. The only solution is to summon the
courage to honor your own judgment, frightening though that might be in the beginning.

## May 19

If you take the position that your happiness is primarily in your own hands, you give yourself enormous power. You are not waiting for events or other people to make you happy. You are not trapped by blame, alibis, or self-pity. You are free to look at the options available in any situation and respond as wisely as you can.

## May 20

If you operate self-responsibly and something goes wrong, your response is not "Someone's got to do something!" but rather, "What can I do? What possibilities for action exist? What needs to be done?"

If you embrace self-responsibility not merely as a personal preference but as a philosophical principle, logically you commit yourself to a profoundly important moral idea. In taking responsibility for your own existence, you implicitly recognize that other human beings are not your servants and do not exist for the satisfaction of your needs. They do not owe you "service." This means you are not entitled to treat other persons merely as a means to your ends, just as you are not a means to their ends. You are not entitled to demand that others work and live for your sake, just as you do not work and live for others. Morally and rationally you are obliged to respect everyone's right to self-interest, just as they are obliged to respect yours. This common understanding is the base of civilized relationships.

## May 22

Blaming is a dead end. What is needed is to focus on solutions, discovering your own resources and mobilizing the will to use them. *What are you willing to do to make your life better?*

Young persons are most likely to learn self-responsibility from adults who exemplify it in their own behavior.

## May 24

Young persons are most likely to learn self-responsibility from parents and teachers who *expect* and *require* it.

## *May 25*

Aside from cases of violent coercion, as when someone points a gun at you, you are responsible for your reactions. No one "makes" you enraged to the point of turning violent. No one "makes" you become sarcastic and abusive. No one "makes" you do the things you are ashamed to take responsibility for.

## May 26

The paradox is that learning self-responsibility leaves you feeling lighter, not heavier, since your life is now in your own hands.

## *May 27*

Some popular ways of avoiding responsibility are pretending to be confused; reaching for an alibi; blaming; and crying, "But that was not in my job description!"

## *May 28*

Self-respecting men and women think about the consequences of their actions—and are willing to take responsibility for them.

## May 29

If you want to learn self-responsibility, meditate on this Spanish proverb: "'Take what you want,' said God, 'and pay for it.'"

## May 30

It is true that people are sometimes hit by adversities beyond their control. But those so affected are better helped when they are awakened to the resources they do possess than when they are told they haven't any.

## May 31

Treat people as if they are self-responsible and they will become self-responsible. Treat people as if they are helpless and they will become helpless. The secret of true kindness is to see the strength in a person that he or she does not yet recognize.

❖ ❖ ❖ ❖ ❖

# June

## June 1

Self-esteem cannot exist without self-assertiveness.

## June 2

It is easy to misunderstand self-assertiveness and to imagine that it means pushing your way to the front of the line, being rude to waiters, acting as if no one but you has needs or rights, or always demanding to be the center of attention. Do not confuse arrogance with intelligent and appropriate self-assertiveness.

## June 3

Self-assertiveness is the willingness to put yourself into reality—your thoughts, your feelings,
your values—in appropriate ways and in appropriate contexts.

## *June 4*

Self-assertiveness should not be confused with mindless rebelliousness. Self-assertiveness without consciousness is tantamount to drunk driving.

## June 5

To practice self-assertiveness is to live authentically, to speak and act from your innermost thoughts and feelings as a way of life—excepting, of course, the obvious circumstances in which you wisely choose not to do so: for example, when confronted by a holdup man.

## June 6

In a class society, when you see a superior talking to an inferior, it is the inferior's eyes that are lowered. It is the slave who looks down, not the master. In the South there was a time when a black man could be beaten for the offense of daring to look at a white woman. *Seeing* is an act of self-assertion and has always been understood as such.

If you pay someone a compliment that genuinely reflects your values, that is self-assertiveness. If you tell a friend that his or her behavior is not acceptable and that you are no longer willing to tolerate it, that also is self-assertiveness.

## June 8

If you express an aesthetic or political conviction in a group without knowing whether anyone will agree or disagree, that is self-assertiveness. So is letting people see your joy and excitement.

## June 9

The willingness to let others see your vulnerability—that, too, is self-assertiveness. You refuse to fake who you are for the sake of an image.

## June 10

Deep and courageous self-assertiveness is letting others hear the music inside you.

Self-assertiveness means treating yourself and your values with decent respect in your encounters with other human beings.

## June 12

The opposite of self-assertiveness is self-abnegation—abandoning or submerging your personal values, judgment, and interests. Some people tell themselves this is a virtue. It is a "virtue" that corrodes self-esteem.

## June 13

Out of fear, out of the desire for approval, out of misguided notions of duty, people surrender themselves—their convictions and their aspirations—every day. There is nothing noble about it. It takes far more courage to fight for your values than to relinquish them.

## June 14

Chances are, when you were young, you were told, in effect, "Listen, kid, here is the news: life is not about you. Life is not about what you want. What you want is not important. Life is about doing what others expect of you." If you accepted this idea, later on you wondered what had happened to your fire. Where had your enthusiasm for living gone?

## June 15

It is naive to think that self-assertiveness is easy. To live self-assertively—which means to live authentically—is an act of high courage. That is why so many people spend the better part of their lives in hiding—from others and also from themselves.

## June 16

It is painful to face the self we know we have never had the integrity to honor and assert.

## June 17

It is humiliating to realize that when you drive yourself underground, when you fake who you are, often you do so for people you do not even like or respect.

## June 18

What is the specter that makes self-assertiveness feel so terrifying? The image of someone frowning in disagreement or disapproval.

## June 19

No one fears death as much as the person who knows he has never lived.

## *June 20*

In a dictatorship people often feel compelled to hide their thoughts and feelings for fear of being arrested or killed. Such fear can be rational. But what does it do to your self-esteem if you live that way in a free country?

## June 21

If you overcome your fear to ask someone for a date, a raise, or help with a project, that is an act of self-assertiveness. You are moving out into life rather than contracting and withdrawing.

❖ ❖ ❖ ❖ ❖

## June 22

To accept the challenge of acquiring a new skill such as mastering the computer or learning to ski or playing chess, especially when the prospect of doing so scares you, is an act of self-assertiveness. You are pushing your boundaries, defying your comfort zone, expanding your territory.

## June 23

One of the hardest expressions of self-asser-tiveness is challenging your limiting beliefs.

## June 24

A bully hides his fears with fake bravado. That is
the opposite of self-assertiveness.

Sometimes, when a man wants to cry, he gets angry; sometimes, when a woman wants to get angry, she cries: two forms of non-self-assertiveness disguised as emotional expressiveness.

## June 26

"Passive-aggressive" is the name psychologists give to people who develop ingenious ways to torture those around them without ever being self-assertive.

## June 27

In an organization self-assertiveness is required not merely to have a good idea but to develop it, fight for it, work to win supporters for it, and do everything in your power to assure its realization.

## June 28

Some people stand and move as if they have no right to the space they occupy. They wonder why others often fail to treat them with respect—not realizing that they have signaled others that it is not necessary to treat them with respect.

## June 29

Persons with good self-esteem tend to be self-assertive. Persons who are self-assertive thereby strengthen their self-esteem. The causality flows in both directions. The relationship is reciprocal.

❖ ❖ ❖ ❖ ❖

## June 30

It is a mistake to look at someone who is self-assertive and say, "It's easy for her, she has good self-esteem." One of the ways you build self-esteem is by being self-assertive when it is not easy to do so. There are always times when self-assertiveness requires courage, no matter how high your self-esteem.

❖

# *July*

❖

## July 1

Self-esteem entails feeling in control of your existence. This feeling requires that you operate purposefully, since it is only through your goals and purposes that you can have any control over your life.

## *July 2*

To exist without purpose is to be at the mercy of the chance encounter, the chance invitation, the chance phone call, the chance event—always being controlled by forces external to oneself.

## July 3

Not all purposes are equal. The key questions about any purpose is this: Does this serve your life and well-being? Is this a purpose you can be proud of?

❖ ❖ ❖ ❖ ❖

## July 4

If you don't know what your goals are, don't be
surprised when you don't attain them.

To live purposefully is to formulate your short-term and long-term goals explicitly. What is your purpose in life? In choosing to get married? In choosing to bring a child into the world? In starting this business? In taking this job? In attending this meeting? In asking this person for a date? In participating in this seminar?

## July 6

To know your purposes is not enough. You need to think through what actions are needed to achieve your purposes. In business this is called having an action plan. Purposes unattached to action plans are not purposes; they are daydreams.

# July 7

"Wouldn't it be nice if—?" isn't a purpose.

## July 8

Once you have formulated your goals and purposes and identified the actions needed to achieve them, you must monitor your behavior to see that it stays in alignment with your stated intentions. It is all too easy to fall off the wagon, to get distracted and sidetracked, to move off in directions unrelated to your goals, purposes, and action plans. Living purposefully entails staying focused on where you are going.

## July 9

What is your purpose in reading this book? What (mental) actions do you need to take to achieve that purpose?

## July 10

To live purposefully, you need to *pay attention to outcomes*. You need to notice whether your actions are producing the results you expected—whether they are bringing you closer to your goal. Perhaps you have a well-formulated purpose, a well thought out action plan, and a pattern of action consistent with your intentions, but the action plan might not be the right one, and you need to go back to the drawing board. The only way to discover this is by paying attention to outcomes. As someone observed, doing more of what doesn't work, doesn't work.

## July 11

A common cause of business failure is seeing that a strategy isn't producing the anticipated results—and responding by going unconscious. The same policy is a common cause of failure in your personal life.

## July 12

You say your goal is to have a happy marriage. What is your plan of action to achieve that result? What do you think must be done to bring about the outcome you desire? And why do you think so? Or do you believe hopes and good intentions will do the trick?

## July 13

You say you want to raise happy, self-confident, and self-responsible children. How much thought have you given to what is required to achieve this result? Have you investigated what you might learn from books on this subject? Why do you think so many parents with the same good intentions as you fail in this endeavor? When you observe that some of your tactics are not successful, do you experiment with other tactics, seek new ideas, or do you stick to the old patterns and blame your children for the poor results?

## July 14

You say you want to rise in your company. What do you do to show that you are worthy of promotion? What is your long-term action plan to advance your career? For example, what new skills are you developing to make yourself more valuable? Or are you merely waiting to be "discovered"?

## July 15

What might you do differently if you were to make being happy your conscious purpose?

## July 16

Daydreams do not produce an experience of
efficacy.

## July 17

No one can feel competent to cope with the challenges of life who has not acquired a capacity for self-discipline.

❖　❖　❖　❖　❖

## July 18

Self-discipline is the ability to organize your behavior over time in the service of specific goals.

## July 19

One of the challenges of effective parenthood or effective teaching is to communicate a respect for the present that does not disregard the future, and a respect for the future that does not disregard the present.

## July 20

A purposeful, self-disciplined life does not mean a life without space or time for rest, relaxation, recreation, and random or even frivolous activity. It merely means that such activities are chosen consciously, with the knowledge that it is safe and appropriate to engage in them.

## July 21

Stressing the practice of living purposefully as essential to fully realized self-esteem is not equivalent to measuring an individual's worth by his or her external achievements. We admire achievements—in ourselves and others—and it is natural and appropriate for us to do so. But that is not the same thing as saying that our achievements are the measure or grounds of our self-esteem. The root of our self-esteem is not our achievements but those internally generated practices that, among other things, *make it possible for us to achieve*.

# July 22

A wealthy businessman in his nineties once said to me, "Let me tell you the great thing about making a fortune, and losing it, and making it again. It's good to get knocked on your back—you learn things you need to know. When I was a young man I thought I was my businesses, bank accounts, and limousines. Then the 1929 depression came and I lost everything and had to begin again. Then I found out that I was not any of my possessions but rather the force inside *that allowed me to acquire them.* And that is something that no external circumstance can take away."

## July 23

At the most basic level, productive work is the application of intelligence to the problem of survival.

❖ ❖ ❖ ❖ ❖

## July 24

A productive purpose to which you give yourself fully and joyfully is one of the great adventures of life. It is a uniquely *human* source of happiness.

## July 25

Do not allow anyone to tell you for what purpose you should live. To be happy and fulfilled, you do need a purpose, but let it rise out of who you are.

## July 26

Energy for which you do not find an appropriate outlet and form of expression can turn into a rage that poisons your soul.

## July 27

Anyone who tells you that your basic purpose on earth is to sacrifice and serve others is not a friend of yours—nor a friend of humanity. Who *is* a friend of yours and of humanity? Anyone who tells you that your life belongs to you and that morality consists of honoring your positive potentialities. The purpose of morality is self-fulfillment, not self-annihilation.

## July 28

Our life is about self-expression, not self-justification. If your goal is to prove you are "enough," the battle is already lost: it was lost on the day you conceded the issue was debatable.

## July 29

A life without a purpose is like a boat without a rudder.

## July 30

One of the most important teachings you can offer a child is the joy of earning a living by doing work one loves.

## July 31

Life is goal-directed. This is a basic fact of biology. But one of the great rewards of being human, in contrast to lower animals, is how many goals we are free to *choose*.

❖

# *August*

❖

## August 1

Integrity is congruence between what you know, what you profess, and what you do.

## *August 2*

Integrity is a key pillar of self-esteem. It is a guardian of mental health. It is the mind being true to itself.

## August 3

When we act in ways that conflict with our judgment of what is appropriate, we lose face in our own eyes.

## August 4

If you do not make any promises and do not profess any principles, you may be accused of other things but not of hypocrisy. To be a hypocrite, you must have something to betray.

## August 5

When a breach of integrity wounds self-esteem,
only an act of integrity can heal it.

## *August 6*

At the simplest level integrity entails some basic questions: Are you honest, reliable, and trustworthy? Do you keep your promises? Do you honor your commitments? Do you do the things you say you admire and avoid the things you say you deplore? Are you fair and just in your dealings with others?

## August 7

Integrity means congruity. Words and behavior match. There are people you know whom you trust and others you don't. If you ask yourself the reason, you will see that congruence is basic. You trust congruity and are suspicious of incongruity.

## *August 8*

Do you want people to trust you and perceive you as a person of integrity? There is no mystery about how to achieve this. Be true to your word. Keep your commitments.

## August 9

If you act against what you yourself believe is right, if your actions clash with your professed values, then you are acting against your own judgment—you are betraying your own mind. How can self-esteem not be affected by this?

## August 10

One of the great self-deceptions—and one of the great foolishnesses—is to tell yourself, Only I will know. Only you will know that you are a liar; only you will know you deal unethically with people who trust you; only you will know you have no intention of honoring your promise. *Whose knowledge or judgment do you imagine is more important?* It is precisely your own ego from which there is no escape.

## *August 11*

Most people do not erode their self-esteem over big issues but over small ones, little acts of betrayal and hypocrisy forgotten (repressed) very quickly. But the computer in your subconscious mind forgets nothing. It records your spiritual profit and loss. The balance sheet reflects your present level of self-esteem—and sends you the information via your emotions.

## *August 12*

The desire for self-esteem without integrity is like the desire for wealth without effort—a longing for the unearned.

## August 13

What is guilt? It is moral self-reproach—I did wrong when it was possible to have done otherwise.

## *August 14*

Rationally, there cannot be guilt where there is neither choice nor responsibility.

## August 15

The idea of original sin—of guilt with no possibility of innocence, no freedom of choice, no alternatives—inherently militates against self-esteem. The very notion of guilt without volition or responsibility is an assault on reason as well as on morality. Sin is not original, it is originated—like virtue.

If you have done something you know to be wrong, if you feel guilty about it and wish to correct it, there are usually five steps you should take: (1) Acknowlege the fact that it is you who have taken the particular action. Face and accept the full reality of what you have done, without denial or disavowal. Acknowledge, accept, and take responsibility. Do not say, It really wasn't me. (2) Seek to understand why you did what you did. Understand where you were coming from. (3) If others are involved, as they often are, acknowledge explicitly to the relevant persons the harm you have done. Convey your understanding of the consequences of your behavior. Convey your understanding of how they have been affected. (4) Take any and all actions that might make amends for or minimize the harm you have done. (5) Firmly commit yourself to acting differently in the future.

## *August 17*

Some people would rather suffer guilt than take the actions necessary to eliminate the guilt.

There is no virtue in guilt. The question is: What are you going to do about it? If you avoid that question, not only is guilt not a virtue, it is a cop-out.

## August 19

It is easy enough to say, Be true to your values. But what if your values are irrational? Or what if the virtues to which you have committed yourself are so inimical to human nature that they cannot be practiced consistently? Be careful of what you accept as your code of morality. Think carefully about whether its tenets serve your life and well-being. Exercise critical judgment. Realize how much is at stake—your life, your happiness, your self-esteem.

## August 20

If we see that our values are leading us towards destruction, clearly it is time to question our values.

## *August 21*

Without self-responsibility, we cannot practice integrity—we will not choose our moral code mindfully.

## August 22

As spiritual advice, "Follow your bliss" is well-intentioned, perhaps, but clearly inadequate. If one wished to reduce morality to a single sentence (which is a dubious endeavor), one had better say, "Live consciously; take responsibility for your choices and actions; respect the rights of others; and follow your bliss." But, of course, life is much too complex for moral one-liners, except insofar as they serve as reminders of basic principles.

## *August 23*

In a society where political figures, religious leaders, business associates, corporate heads, and other public personalities hold themselves to high standards of morality, it is relatively easier for an average person to practice integrity than it is in a society where corruption, cynicism, and amorality are the norm. In the latter kind of society, an individual is likely to feel that the quest for personal integrity is futile and unrealistic—unless he or she is extraordinarily independent and autonomous, inner-directed rather than outer-directed.

## August 24

The challenge for people today—and it is not an easy one—is to maintain high personal standards even while feeling that one is living in a moral sewer.

The more you live consciously, the more you trust your mind and respect your worth; and if you trust your mind and respect your worth, it feels natural to live consciously. The more you practice integrity, the more you enjoy good self-esteem; and if you enjoy good self-esteem, it feels natural to practice integrity.

## August 26

When integrity comes to feel like your natural state, you feel dishonesty on your part as disturbing, and you feel a thrust to resolve the dissonance and restore an inner sense of moral cleanliness.

## *August 27*

Here's a test for the feeling of integrity: Are you proud of your choices and actions? For most people it's a question more often avoided than confronted. But what an opportunity for growth the question offers!

## *August 28*

Some people admire men and women of integrity; others are made nervous—they experience an unspoken sense of reproach, not knowing it lies within themselves.

## August 29

When your own good opinion matters more to you than someone else's, you have the foundation for self-esteem.

❖ ❖ ❖ ❖ ❖

## August 30

Self-esteem is not a luxury: it is a profound
spiritual need.

## August 31

The virtues that self-esteem asks of us—living consciously, self-acceptance, self-responsibility, self-assertiveness, purposefulness, integrity—are also the virtues that life asks of us.

# September

## September 1

The first love affair you must consummate successfully is the love affair with yourself. Only then are you ready for a romantic relationship.

## September 2

When a man and woman encounter each other in romantic love, seeking union, seeking fusion, seeking the experience of the most intimate contact, they come to each other from a context of aloneness. An understanding of this fact is essential. Paradoxically, if you wish to understand romantic love, you must begin by understanding aloneness, the universal condition of us all.

## September 3

We are all parts of one universe, true enough.
We stand within an almost infinite network of
relationships. Yet each of us is a single point of
consciousness, a unique event, a private, unre-
peatable world. This is the essence of our aloneness.

## September 4

Without an "I" who loves, what is the meaning of love? First, there must be a self—then, the exquisite joy of one self encountering another.

## September 5

To love a human being is to know and love his or her *person*. This communion presupposes the ability to see, and with reasonable clarity. Love without sight is not love but self-deception.

## September 6

All of us experience who we are in the context of our relationships.

All positive interactions with other human beings involve, to some degree, the experience of visibility—that is, the experience of being seen and understood.

## September 8

The first desire of romantic love is to see and to feel seen—to exchange the experience of psychological or spiritual visibility.

## September 9

Whoever allows us to feel deeply seen holds a powerful grip on our emotions. This is one of the reasons people can form such strong emotional attachments with their psychotherapists.

## September 10

Romantic love is a passionate spiritual-emotional-sexual attachment between two people that reflects a high regard for each other's value. Romantic love entails mutual admiration.

## September 11

It is easy to confuse romantic love with loneliness, need, neurotic dependency, or sexual attraction in the absence of mutual esteem. And for this reason, when such relationships crash or lead to little but mutual torture, "romantic love" often gets the blame

## *September 12*

Romantic love is an expression not only of esteem for the other but also esteem for yourself. A healthy ego is a precondition of healthy love.

## September 13

Everyone knows this cliché: If you don't love yourself, it's difficult to love another. Less well understood is the other half of the story: If you don't love yourself, it's very difficult to accept the love of another—very difficult to believe in its reality, very difficult to let it fully in—because such love clashes with your self-concept.

## *September 14*

If you enjoy a fundamental sense of efficacy and worth, and if, as a consequence, you feel lovable as a human being, you have a basis for appreciating and loving others. You are not trapped in feelings of deficiency. You have a surplus of life within you, an emotional wealth that you can channel into loving.

## *September 15*

Without respect for and enjoyment of who you are, you have very little to give emotionally. You tend to see others primarily as sources of approval or disapproval. You do not appreciate them in their own right. But if you can learn to do so—and this is something that can be learned—you grow in self-esteem. And you begin to feel less needy.

## September 16

People high in self-esteem long to feel admiration; people low in self-esteem long to feel accepted.

## September 17

Being romantic means *treating the relationship as important*, behaving in ways that underscore its importance.

## September 18

The fact that you and your partner love each other does not guarantee that you will be able to create a joyful and rewarding relationship. Love per se does not ensure maturity and wisdom; yet without these qualities love is in jeopardy. Love does not automatically teach communication skills, effective methods of conflict resolution, or the art of integrating your love into the rest of your existence; yet the absence of such knowledge can lead to the death of love. Love does not produce self-esteem; it may reinforce and nurture it, but it cannot create it; still, without self-esteem love is difficult or impossible to sustain.

## September 19

Every love affair is a private universe.

A successful relationship between a man and a woman rests on fundamental similarities between them and on complementary differences. Harmony in love requires a partner with whom we enjoy essential affinities in values and sense of life. But the excitement we also hope to find requires that there be some differences in personality development, in skills, in styles of being and doing—complementary differences, obviously, not antagonistic ones (like intelligence and its opposite). This special combination is necessary to make two people right for each other.

## *September 21*

In romantic love the most basic similarity that makes love possible is that both people are human; the most basic complementary difference that produces excitement is the fact that one is a man and the other a woman.

## September 22

If you do not feel deserving of happiness, consciously or subconsciously, or if you have accepted the idea that happiness is somehow wrong or cannot last, you will not respond appropriately when happiness comes knocking at your door in the form of romantic love. No matter how much you may have waited and cried, you will not welcome love when it arrives—you will find a way to sabotage it. What a challenge to resist this temptation! What an opportunity for true spiritual growth and transformation—to defy your negative feelings and honor the gift that life offers you!

## *September 23*

One of the pleasures of romantic love that nurtures the relationship is talking about what you
enjoy and appreciate in each other.

❖   ❖   ❖   ❖   ❖

## September 24

When your lover conveys that you are a source
of pleasure, you feel loved.

## September 25

Experts at seduction know how to make another person feel visible.

## September 26

To nurture another person is to accept him or her unreservedly, to respect his or her sovereignty, to support his or her growth toward self-actualization, and to *care* about his or her thoughts, feelings, and wants. Ideally, nurturing is a reciprocal process. If you care only about your own needs and not those of your partner, you relate as a child to a parent, not as an equal to an equal. In romantic love independent equals do not drain or exploit each other; they nurture each other. Mutual nurturing is one of the characteristics of happy relationships.

## September 27

To nurture is to love not only your partner's strength but also his or her fragility, not only that within your partner that is powerful but also that which is delicate, not only that which is grown-up but also that which is young.

In successful romantic love, there is a unique depth of absorption by and fascination with the being and personality of the partner. Hence, for each there can be a powerful experience of visibility—which creates a powerful bond. It is supremely important to know how to make your partner feel visible: seen, understood, appreciated.

## September 29

In love, the self is celebrated, not denied, abandoned, or sacrificed.

## September 30

What you love is the embodiment of your values in another human being—hardly an act of self-abnegation. Love is not selfless. Ask yourself whether you want your lover to caress you unselfishly, with no pleasure or gratification, or whether you want you want your lover to caress you because it is a joy for him or her to do so. Ask yourself whether you want your partner to spend time alone with you and to experience doing so as an act of *self-sacrifice*—or whether you want your partner to experience doing so as glory. And if it's glory that you want your partner to feel, if you want your partner to experience joy in your presence, to feel excitement, ardor, passion, fascination, delight—then stop talking about selfless love as a noble ideal. Would anyone with even a shred of self-respect say, I want you to love me *selflessly*?" It is a very strange "spirituality" that identifies love with selflessness. The great compliment of love is that your personal concept of self-interest expands to include the happiness and well-being of your partner. Your partner's joy and fulfillment matter to you selfishly. And when your partner sees that attitude in you, he or she feels truly loved.

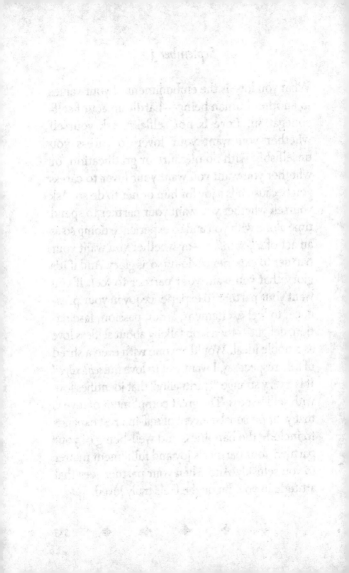

# October

Your desire for love from others is inseparable from your desire for visibility. Think about it. If someone professed love for you but when talking about what he or she found lovable named characteristics you did not think you possessed, did not especially admire, and could not personally relate to, you would hardly feel nourished or loved. You do not merely wish to be loved; you wished to be loved for reasons that are personally meaningful to you and that are congruent with your perception of yourself. Celebrities and beautiful people in general often feel invisible in spite of having numerous admirers precisely because they recognize that their fans are in love with their own fantasy of the person, not the real person.

## October 2

Romantic love at its best: in loving your partner, you encounter yourself. A lover ideally reacts to you as, in effect, you would react to yourself in the person of another. Thus, you perceive your self through your lover's reaction. You perceive your own person through its consequences in the consciousness—and, as a result, the behavior—of your partner.

## October 3

In feeling visible to your lover, you discover new aspects of who you are. Love stimulates self-discovery. That is one source of its excitement.

## October 4

The desire for psychological visibility is not the same as the desire to be validated by someone. The desire to be seen and understood is not the same as the desire to be approved of. The desire to have your goodness recognized and perceived is different from waiting to find out from someone else whether you are good.

## October 5

The desire for sexual as well as psychological union is part of romantic love. Through the exchange of intense pleasure, lovers celebrate life, self, and each other in a single act.

## October 6

Pleasure allows us to experience *life* as a value and *yourself* as a value. There is no knowledge more precious than that of the value of life and of self. And sexual joy at its most intense provides this knowledge—not abstractly, but with the vividness and intensity of direct sensory perception.

## October 7

Sex is unique among pleasures in its integration of body and mind, or body and spirit—providing, of course, that you can take pride in your choice of partner. When your choice is a source of shame or embarrassment, that is another story entirely.

## October 8

In sex more than in any other activity you experience the fact that you are an end in yourself and that the purpose of life is happiness.

## October 9

If sex involves an act of self-celebration; if, in sex, you desire the freedom to be spontaneous, to be emotionally open and uninhibited, to assert your right to pleasure, and to flaunt your pleasure in your own being—then the person you most desire is the person with whom you feel freest to be who you are, the person who you (consciously or subconsciously) regard as an appropriate psychological mirror, the person who reflects your deepest view of yourself and of life.

## October 10

A healthy masculinity or femininity is the consequence or expression of an affirmative response
to your own sexual nature. This entails a strong,
enthusiastic awareness of your own sexuality; a
positive (fearless and guiltless) response to the
phenomenon of sex; a disposition to experience
sex as an *expression* of the self rather than as
something alien or darkly incomprehensible; a
positive and self-valuing response to your own
body; an enthusiastic appreciation of the body
of the opposite sex; a capacity for freedom,
spontaneity, and delight in the sexual encounter.

## October 11

The essence of romantic love is this: I see you as a person, and because you are what you are, I love and desire you—for my happiness in general and my sexual happiness in particular.

## October 12

Fascination, attraction, passion may be born at first sight. Love cannot. Love requires time. But later, looking back, if your initial feelings are supported and reinforced by subsequent knowledge and experience, it can *feel* that love began at first sight.

## October 13

Often you are most intolerant in your lover of those qualities you have disowned in yourself. So paying attention to what angers you or makes you impatient can be a doorway leading to deepened self-awareness.

An immature woman looks at her lover and, deep in her psyche, there is the thought: "My father made me feel rejected; you will take his place and give me what he failed to give me. I will create a home for you and cook your meals and bear your children—I will be your good little girl." An immature man looks at his bride and thinks, "Now I am a married man; I am grown up; I have responsibilities—just like Father. I will work hard, I will be your protector, I will take care of you—just as Father did with Mother. Then he and you and everyone will see that I am a good boy."

## October 15

On one level it is true enough to say that a characteristic of immature love is that the man and woman do not perceive each other realistically; fantasies and projections take the place of clear vision. Yet on a deeper level, often they do know whom they have chosen. They pretend to be blind—so that the drama of later suffering can play itself out and they can fulfill the disappointment they always knew was their "destiny."

## October 16

To take responsibility for our life and happiness, we need to relinquish the belief that frustration and defeat are our natural and inevitable fate.

Individuals high in self-esteem are usually attracted to others high in self-esteem; those with medium self-esteem usually seek out others with medium self-esteem; and likewise for those with low self-esteem. In such cases attraction does not refer to a momentary sexual response but to the enduring attachment we are likely to call "love."

## October 18

The first requirement of happiness in romantic love is a vision of yourself that contains the *rightness* of being loved, the *naturalness* of being loved, the *appropriateness* of being loved.

People who love themselves do not find it incomprehensible that others should love them. They are able to *allow* others to love them. Their love has ease and grace.

The tragedy of too many people is that they cannot allow happiness just to be there; they cannot leave it alone. Their sense of who they are and of what their destiny is cannot accommodate happiness. So they are driven to find ways to sabotage it.

## October 21

Some people have a view of self and of the universe that obliges them to *struggle* for happiness, to yearn for happiness—"some time in the future"—perhaps next year or the year after that. But not now. Not at this moment. Not here. Here and now is too terrifyingly close, too terrifyingly immediate. They suffer from *happiness anxiety*.

Romantic love is for grown-ups; it is not for children. It is not for children in a literal sense or in a psychological sense: not for those who, regardless of age, still exerience themselves as children. Romantic love requires some measure of autonomy.

## October 23

Autonomous men and women have grown beyond the need to prove to anyone that they are good boys or good girls—just as they have grown beyond the need for their spouse or romantic partner to be their mother or father.

❖ ❖ ❖ ❖ ❖

## *October 24*

Autonomous individuals have a greater capacity to roll with the punches, to see the normal frictions of life in perspective, not to get their feelings hurt over trivia; even if they are hurt occasionally, they do not experience such moments as catastrophes.

## October 25

Autonomous lovers respect their partner's need to follow his or her own destiny, to be alone sometimes, to be preoccupied sometimes, *not* to be thinking about the relationship sometimes, to be concerned about other vital matters that may not involve the partner in any direct sense, such as work, personal unfolding and evolution, and personal developmental needs. Give this freedom to yourself as well as to the person you love.

Only when you stop fighting the fact of your ultimate aloneness are you ready for romantic love.

So much of the joy of love—so much that nurtures love—has to do with showing and sharing who you are. To be afraid of self-disclosure is to be afraid of love. Mutual self-disclosure opens the door to many of the most precious values romantic love can offer.

## October 28

When your partner is in pain over something, often the greatest gift you can offer is just to let your partner talk, and for you just to listen, just to be there, just to be available, and to convey your understanding of your partner's feelings without any obligation to say something brilliant, produce a solution, or cheer your partner up. Often merely expressing the problem to a caring listener fosters healing.

Relationships are not destroyed by honest expressions of anger (those that avoid character assassination). But relationships die every day as a consequence of unexpressed anger. The repression of anger, the refusal to discuss grievances, kills love, kills sex, kills passion.

## October 30

The willingness to share your pain, your fear, and your anger—and to be open to the same from your partner—serves the growth of romantic love. Unwillingness to do so subverts its growth.

## October 31

Romantic love is not a fantasy or delusion, but it requires more of you—in terms of spiritual maturity—than anyone ever told you.

# *November*

## November 1

To share a life with someone means far more than merely living in the same house or keeping company. It means sharing your inner world, all that pertains to the self. Is this something you are willing to do? It is better to decide before the marriage than afterward.

## November 2

If you are afraid to know what you want or to express it unambiguously to your partner, to take responsibility for it, you might end up blaming your partner. You might feel hurt and resentment over your partner's lack of "sensitivity." You aren't a mind reader? Neither is your partner.

## November 3

Some people justify their cynicism about romantic love by pointing out that romantic love doesn't last. But for most people, *no passion lasts*. Why single out romantic love? It is a rare individual who knows how to nurture and sustain his or her excitement about anything. Doing so is an achievement to be admired.

✤ ✤ ✤ ✤ ✤

## November 4

Some people are afraid of excitement—their own or anyone else's. *Never marry anyone who is not a friend to your excitement.*

## November 5

There is no aphrodisiac as powerful as authentic communication.

## November 6

Through the giving and receiving of sexual pleasure, lovers continually reaffirm their joy in
each other.

## November 7

Men and women need each other. That should make them friends. Too often, however, it makes them enemies because of the fear and anticipation of being hurt.

## November 8

Fully to surrender to love can be terrifying. But it is the price life asks in exchange for the possibility of ecstasy.

## November 9

If you do not know how to deal sensitively and intelligently with your lover, taking a second lover will probably not enhance your wisdom. It will merely expand the area of your incompetence.

## November 10

Life is motion. Not to move forward is to move backward. If you are not evolving, you are decaying. If you and your partner are not growing together, you are dying together.

There are many complex reasons for falling in love with someone. Not all of them are self-evident. One of the pleasures of lovers is seeking to identify on deeper and deeper levels the traits that inspire and excite them in each other. The process can go on for years and can be a source of increasing pleasure and intimacy.

## November 12

A psychologist of my acquaintance announced, "Romantic love *requires* blindness. Passion dies in the light." "Do you mean," I answered, "that no one who really understands you can possibly be in love with you? Maybe so. But why lay that charge against the whole human race?"

## November 13

When you enter a love relationship, you do so with certain explicit wants and expectations. Do you know what yours are? Do you know what your partner's are? Do you feel a responsibility to give that which you would like to receive (or its equivalent)?

## November 14

Grown-ups carry their own weight—at work
and in marriage.

## November 15

Each person brings to a relationship certain
assets and shortcomings. Do you know what
yours are? What do you bring to a relationship
that your partner is likely to find valuable? What
do you bring that your partner might find difficult or troublesome? Do you feel an obligation to know (or discover) the answers to these
questions?

If you talk to people who have remained deeply in love over many years, you will find that they are mindful of their partners. Their love is mentally active. Mental passivity is the enemy of passion. Sleepwalking is not conducive to romantic love.

## November 17

Loving consciously does not mean subjecting your relationship to endless analysis. It means something much simpler: paying attention. Noticing. This requires *presence*.

## November 18

If you find yourself in conflict with your partner, notice how the conflict is handled. When friction erupts, who does what? Is the focus on finding a solution or finding fault? On understanding or blaming or defending? Are differences approached in a spirit of benevolence or of fear and hostility? What has priority—protecting the relationship or self-justification (proving yourself "right")? If estrangement sets in, who typically makes the first move to overcome it? What is the other partner doing in the meantime?

## *November 19*

Self-esteem supports the success of love. The success of love supports self-esteem.

## November 20

Whoever expresses an opinion about romantic love makes a personal confession. We speak out of what we have lived. Cynicism, for instance, is as much a statement about yourself as about anyone else.

Sometimes when people speak about romantic love they are really speaking about infatuation, which is quite another story. While love embraces the person as a whole, infatuation is the result of focusing on one or two aspects and reacting as if that were the whole. You see a beautiful face and assume it is the image of a beautiful soul. You see that this person treats you kindly and you assume the two of you have significant affinities. You discover that you have important values in one area and conclude you must be soul mates. When you awaken from the dream, it is hard to remember where your mind could have been.

It is sometimes argued that since so many couples suffer feelings of disenchantment shortly after marriage, the experience of romantic love must be a delusion. Yet many people experience disenchantment during their careers somewhere along the line, but it is not commonly suggested that the pursuit of a fulfilling career is a mistake. Many people experience some degree of disenchantment in their children, but it is not commonly supposed that the desire to have children and to be happy about them is inherently immature and neurotic. Instead, it is generally recognized that achieving happiness in one's career or success in child-rearing is more difficult than is ordinarily supposed. Precisely the same conclusion should be drawn about romantic love.

## November 23

Among the many rewards of love is the opportunity to share your excitement and be nourished by the excitement of another.

Sometimes pain is easier to bear alone than happiness.

There is a reason why dictatorships set themselves against romantic love, labeling it petty and selfish—as dramatized, for example, in Orwell's *1984*. Romantic love is intrinsically individualistic.

## November 26

For "I" to become "we" and yet to remain "I,"
is one of the great challenges of marriage.

## *November 27*

There has never been a time when the word *love* was used quite so loosely as it is today. People say they "love" everyone. They say *everyone* is supposed to love everyone. However, love by its very nature entails a process of selection, of discrimination. Love is your response to that which represents your deepest values. Love is a response to distinctive characteristics possessed by some beings but not by all. If love between adults did not imply admiration, if it did not imply an appreciation of traits and qualities that the recipient of love possesses, what meaning or significance would love have, and why would anyone consider it desirable? You can offer most people respect and good will. You cannot offer them love. But you can claim to.

❖ ❖ ❖ ❖ ❖

"Loving everyone" sounds suspiciously like spiritual promiscuity—the abandonment of all standards.

Many years ago, early in our relationship, my wife, Devers, said something that impressed me profoundly. "You are very kind, generous, and caring—when you stop long enough in what you are doing for it to occur to you. What you have never learned is *the discipline of kindness*. This means kindness that is not a matter of mood or convenience. It means kindness as a basic way of functioning. It is in you as a potential, but it doesn't happen without consciousness and discipline." "The discipline of kindness"—I have learned to love that phrase. When I mention it in lectures, everyone seems instantly to know what it means—just as, I suspect, you do now.

Romantic love is not a distraction from spiritual growth but one of the paths by which it may be attained. It tests spiritual maturity in unique ways. It presents unique challenges to your honesty and authenticity. It can be easier to assume the role of guru and address thousands of people from the insulated safety of a lecture platform than to encounter in your living room one human being who might love and respect you but who faces you as an equal and is not afraid to challenge your judgment, question some of your actions, pull you back when you have gone too far, and, when necessary, tell you to "come off it."

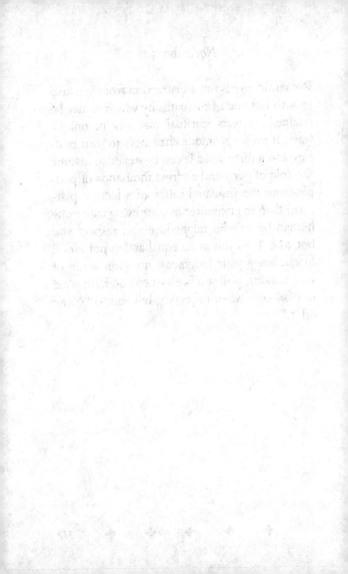

# December

## December 1

The more rapid the rate of change, the more dangerous it is to live mechanically, relying on routines of belief and behavior that might be irrelevant or obsolete.

## December 2

Everyone operates more consciously in some areas than in others. People might bring great consciousness to their work and very little to personal relationships—or vice versa. They might think far more clearly about their careers than about their political beliefs—or vice versa. They might maintain a sharp mental focus in matters pertaining to their health but a more diffuse focus in matters pertaining to ethics or religion—or vice versa. To say that a person is not living at an adequate level of consciousness is to say that that there are aspects of his or her life where the range of action exceeds the range of thought.

## December 3

Sometimes there is no choice but to act instantly with no time for reflection. It is an act of consciousness to recognize such moments and take your chances—and know that you will live (or possibly die) with the consequences of your actions.

## December 4

Whether your focus is on preserving and strengthening family ties in a world of increasingly unstable relationships, gaining access to a decent job, growing and evolving as a person, or guiding a company through the stormy seas of a fiercely competitive global marketplace— whether your goals are material, emotional, or spiritual—the price of success is the same: thinking, learning. To be asleep at the wheel— to rely only on the known, familiar, and automatized—is to invite disaster.

To arrive at a contradiction is to know that you have made an error. To persist in a contradiction is to short-circuit your mind.

## December 6

When you live consciously, you do not evade facts; you do not pretend that by closing your eyes you can annihilate reality.

## December 7

Living consciously reflects the conviction that sight is preferable to blindness; that respecting the facts of reality is more satisfying than defying them; that evasion does not make the unreal real or the real unreal; that it is better to correct your mistakes than to pretend they do not exist; and that the more conscious you are of facts bearing on your life and goals, the more wisely and effectively you can act.

## December 8

If you choose to move through life blindly, you have good reason to be anxious.

## December 9

The quest of reason is for the noncontradictory integration of experience.

❖   ❖   ❖   ❖   ❖

## December 10

No other gift to a young person can equal that of teaching the intimate relationship that exists between rationality and self-esteem—between consciousness and efficacy.

## December 11

Whether in the workplace or in personal relationships, success belongs to those who are willing to take responsibility for attaining their desires—those who respond to life actively rather than passively.

❖ ❖ ❖ ❖ ❖

## December 12

To those who have fully experienced the joy of operating consciously, the feeling is I = consciousness = aliveness.

## December 13

It is not a sin to have an impulse to avoid some painful fact. But learn to manage such impulses. Do not be ruled by them.

## December 14

If you bring 5 percent more awareness to your work tomorrow, or to your most important relationship, what might you do differently? Are you willing to find out?

## *December 15*

If you give 5 percent more respect to your deepest needs and wants, what might you do differently? Are you willing to try it and see what you might discover?

## December 16

If morality—or spirituality—means anything, it means, first and foremost, a commitment to be aware.

## December 17

It is cruel and misleading to tell people that all they need to do to have self-esteem is decide to love themselves. Self-esteem is built by practices, not by emotions.

❖ ❖ ❖ ❖ ❖

## December 18

When they lack self-esteem, people often try to create *pseudo*-self-esteem—a pretense at self-confidence and self-respect they do not actually feel. The act is chiefly for oneself.

## December 19

The errors you are willing to confront become the rungs of a ladder leading to higher self-esteem.

## December 20

You have a right to your feelings. Your feelings are there to tell you something, but they are not infallible guides to behavior.

## December 21

As you grow in self-esteem, your face, manner, and way of talking and moving will naturally project the pleasure you take in being alive.

❖ ❖ ❖ ❖ ❖

## December 22

It does not take intelligence to suffer. It often takes intelligence to be happy. It takes the wisdom to know how to make oneself happy.

## December 23

Anyone who really loves you wants you to be authentic. And anyone who doesn't want you to be authentic doesn't really love you.

## December 24

Live self-assertively. Bring into the world that which you think, value, and feel. Do not consign yourself to the unexpressed and unlived.

## December 25

The real basic power of an individual isn't what he or she knows, it's the ability to think and learn and face new challenges.

## December 26

Healthy self-esteem isn't only about your ability to cope with the challenges of life, but also about your right to enjoy the rewards—your right to be happy and to feel pride in what you have accomplished.

## December 27

People who are intelligently ambitious are always looking at the wider picture. They look for opportunities to contribute. They look for what needs to be done.

## December 28

The world belongs to the people who are willing to take responsibility.

## December 29

You are not likely to bring out the best in people or nurture their creativity if every time you hear about their problems you instantly offer a solution. Encourage people to look for their own solutions—and project the knowledge that they are capable of doing so.

## December 30

Set goals that don't feel all that easy, that challenge you, stimulate you, and give you a chance to stretch and push yourself. That is where the power of growth lies.

## December 31

Self-esteem is your reputation with yourself.

# About the Author

With a Ph.D. in psychology and a background in philosophy, Nathaniel Branden is a practicing psychotherapist in Los Angeles and, in addition, does corporate consulting all over the world, conducting seminars, workshops, and conferences on the application of self-esteem principles and technology to the challenges of modern business. He is the author of many books, including *The Six Pillars of Self-Esteem, Taking Responsibility,* and *The Art of Living Consciously.* His writings have been translated into fourteen languages, and there are more than 3 million copies of his books in print.

In addition to his in-person practice, he consults via telephone worldwide. He can be reached through his Los Angeles office at:

*P.O. Box 2609*
*Beverly Hills, CA 90213*
*Telephone: (310) 274-6361*
*Fax: (310) 271-6808*
*E-mail: NathanielBranden@Compuserve.com*
*Website: http://www.nathanielbranden.net*

❖    ❖    ❖    ❖    ❖    *411*

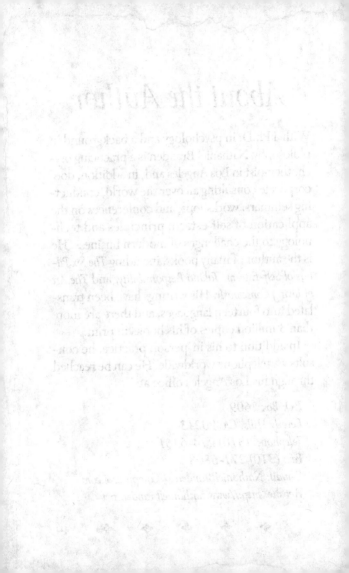